Praise for *Cleave*

"Adoptees might spend their lives wondering 'Who Am I?' but so do birth mothers who surrender their children. With unflinching honesty, Holly Pelesky considers the confounding nature of 'love in absence' that characterizes the relationship between her and the child she didn't raise. Nuanced, compassionate, and fearless, *Cleave* confronts the complexity of the human heart."
—Jody Keisner, author of *Under My Bed and Other Essays*

"In spare chapters that read like epistolary confessions to the daughter she placed up for adoption, Pelesky grapples with what it means to choose a life, a love. With sharp, lyrical sentences and the raw reveal of her prose, it is clear she lives her life the way she delivers lines on the page: with unflinching honesty and careful intention. *Cleave* is a masterful look into what it means to be a mother, a daughter, a wife—but most of all, how to fall in love with yourself."
—Dina L. Relles, editor at *Pidgeonholes*

"Driven by a razor-sharp voice piping with insight, power, and grace, Pelesky's *Cleave* will empty the ashtray in your heart and replenish it with kisses and hard candies. You will put this book down only to come up for air!"
—Jessica Anne, author of *A Manual for Nothing*

"A powerful new addition to the memoir genre, perfectly balancing formal innovation with heartbreaking and moving reflections on what it means to be a mother and how to make a life that is truly one's own."
—Joe Neary, *Chicago Review of Books*

Cleave

Holly Pelesky

Autofocus Books
Easton, Pennsylvania

©Holly Pelesky, 2022
All rights reserved.

Published by Autofocus Books
autofocusbooks.com

2nd edition (2026)

Essay/Memoir
ISBN: 978-1-957392-09-7

Cover design by Amy Wheaton
Library of Congress Control Number: 2022940889

[kleev]

1. v. to part or split
2. v. to remain attached, as to an idea, hope, memory

For Grace

Table of Contents

I

Say You're Pregnant 3
Replacement Dog 7
Nourishment 9
Christmas 2005 13
About Your Biological Father 17
Pulp in My Hand 21

II

Honeymoon 27
14 Emerald Lane 31
What I Kept 37
Active Mothering 41
But on Another Note 45
About Chains 47
Ten 57
Now That I'm Being Honest 61
Leaving 67

III

Bilocation 73
I Keep Meaning to Write About
the Day You Were Born 77
There Was Joy, Too 85
I Want You to Always Know What It Feels
Like to Be Held in Someone's Arms 91

Cleave

Say You're Pregnant

Say you just found out you're pregnant, after your second time having sex.

You were raised to be a virgin until marriage, then a wife, then a mother.

When you hear the voicemail from your brother saying, "Mom and dad know," you climb into your car and decide you will drive far away, change your name maybe, work in a filling station in Wyoming or Montana or South Dakota. But the January mountains stop you. You turn the car around.

You sit on the couch and cry when your mom asks how this happened. You explain what you've been up to at college: not Bible studies and church services but drinking your nights away after working doubles at the restaurant.

She asks you what it's like to be drunk. She's never had even a sip of alcohol. Tell her it's like being someone else. But don't tell her that it's like being someone closer to yourself, someone you weren't raised to be.

She says you're moving back in with her for the duration of your pregnancy. And since you will be living at her house again, you will be going to church each week. You don't resist, even though you want to. You've disobeyed enough already.

You post your apartment on Craigslist, quit your job, fax your résumé to a restaurant close to your parents' house. It doesn't take long until you run out of money. You get a job at a café that serves quiche and sandwiches and mochas. You work weekend mornings so you no longer have to bother with church. Mostly, the clientele is people visiting dying loved ones in hospice next door.

Your mother expects you to keep the baby, to stay living at home, to raise it with her help. The adoption agency gives you a second batch of profiles and there is a couple you know immediately is the right one.

You keep working at the café, your belly growing and growing, your belt dropping lower and lower beneath it. This small thing of making lattes and slicing cakes and delivering quiche to tables of grieving people makes you feel useful.

You find out your baby is a girl. Tears slip from your cheeks on the examination table while the ultrasound technician talks excitedly about your baby as if you'll keep her.

The adoption agency throws you a shower. Your college roommate, writing professor, a waitress you work with, and your daughter's mother show up and give you gifts.

It's getting hot; it's summer, and you're huge with child and bloat.

You show up to the hospital on time. After a workday of labor, she is born. A nurse brings her to you, swaddled, only her face peeking out. Her red blotchy cheeks look like yours.

You try not to cry.

You cry, even though you tried so hard not to.

When you watch your daughter's mother hold her, you look away.

You count down the hours, no the minutes, until it's over: the torturous forty-eight hours you have to change your mind and keep the baby.

You tell your daughter's parents they can name her.

They pick *Grace*.

You call her Gracie instead. Like she's yours. Like you have any say in who she becomes.

Ten days after she is born, you move away. On your way out of the state, you stop at her house over the Cascade Mountains. She's so much bigger already, her cheeks full. She has reddish skin and blond hair and blue eyes, just like you. And you love her.

Say you will live without each other.

Say you climb into your Saturn loaded down with your belongings and back down the drive.

Say you wave.

Say you leave.

Say you leave.

Say you leave.

Say you've left your daughter.

Clutching the wheel, you convince yourself you'll try to go on.

You don't know what the hell that means.
But say you try.

Replacement Dog

People brought items that wouldn't remind me of you, even though you were there, in the room, beneath my black tank top with sequins that rubbed my arms raw. You were kicking. I got some books probably, maybe candles. The only thing I remember is this big ceramic dog bowl painted over with white bones. I received it because my plan was to move halfway across the country after you were born to start a life of my own. I would get a dog. I would need a dog. I dreamed of a chocolate lab; I would rub my hands through his coat and he would lick my hand while music played in my empty apartment. I would get a retractable leash and take him on runs.

There were only two apartments in Omaha, Nebraska that accepted dogs over fifty pounds. I reserved one. I was putting all hope of future wellbeing in that imaginary dog. I would transfer my emotions from you to him. It would be that easy, that transactional.

When I got to Omaha from Puyallup, I stayed on my friend Marie's couch until my apartment was ready. My Saturn was packed to the gills in the parking lot with clothes and books and trinkets of the life I'd left behind. We looked in the classifieds for dogs. There were beagle puppies. We went—just to look—I got one. I named him Tucker, a name I had picked when I was five months pregnant with you and told your parents they could choose your name. When I wanted desperately to name someone.

I left Tucker alone in my bare apartment while I worked lunches and dinners at the Olive Garden. I came home to ripped-up DVD cases and puddles of pee. Tucker cried all night. He was draining me with his needs, guilting me for not being there. I had adopted him away from his family for what? To leave him crying alone without so much as a couch to curl up on. We didn't bond. He never nestled into the crook of my arm. We didn't run together or walk anywhere. We both lay alone on the floor in the fetal position, curled into commas, shrinking into periods.

I gave Tucker away to a boy at the Olive Garden. He was renamed Delta, became a frat dog licking beer out of Solo cups, pot exhaled into his giant eyes by laughing stoners. And I am empty, like my apartment. So far this year, I graduated college and gave away my baby and then my dog. I'm spending the rest of it lying on the floor, reading poetry books after my restaurant shifts, scribbling my thoughts into a notebook. I see everything from the ground, without anything to elevate myself. The blue dog bowl sits on the floor next to my refrigerator, unfilled.

Nourishment

My sister Amber and I eat bagels slathered in cream cheese and loaded with Dagwood's turkey for my first Thanksgiving on my own. She caught a ride from Wisconsin to Nebraska with some girls from her school. We're going to piece together puzzles and play Sequence, just like the old days when we were homeschooled.

Mom sent us a box of chintzy knick-knacks for Thanksgiving. We open it together without anticipation—her gifts are always thematic, never useful—Hershey's minis in their fall wrappings, a little straw pumpkin, a pumpkin spice candle. My ex-boyfriend Steve is here for the occasion; he just sort of settled in. I hand him the candle and tell him to take it to his aunt's where he is spending the holiday.

My apartment is almost filled with furniture now. I was approved for a credit card at one furniture store, then promptly applied for another card with a higher credit limit at a better one. I have two bookshelves, a couch, an entertainment center, dining room and bedroom sets.

A twenty-four pack of Mug Root Beer takes up most of my refrigerator. For dinner, sometimes I make one of those prepackaged pastas, but usually I'm working at the Olive Garden. I often stop at McDonald's on the way to work and get a number eight (chicken sandwich deluxe, crispy). I remember right after you were born your dad brought me a number eight and an Us Weekly magazine. The cover story was about Denise Richards losing the baby weight right away. I didn't, but maybe the root beer isn't helping.

Each day after work, I record my tips on a piece of paper in my green notebook. I make around $450/week between lunch and dinner shifts. Sometimes I write poems in the notebook too. I'm reading local poetry from the library. I have a TV but it's only for watching DVDs. I could get bunny ears for a few free channels, but who cares? *Big Brother* is over any way. Janelle didn't win; she was totally robbed.

On the weekends, I host parties at my apartment. Everyone comes: Marie, Regis, Patrick, Steve, and their drunk friends. I didn't mean to start it back up again with Steve after I dumped him, moved away, and broke his heart. But during one of my parties before the furniture, he was sitting against the wall near this guy Nick that I was kind of seeing. Steve smelled Nick's hair—I mean really inhaled it—and said, "You smell good." I was sitting across the room and I just burst out laughing. I was pretty drunk, sure, but it felt good to laugh.

Plus, Steve knew me before you and that feels important. Like I'm multi-dimensional, maybe, at least to him. Like I was something else before I was a childless mother.

Amber asks if I am dating him and I say no, just friends. I'm not interested because he's kind of a hermit. After Amber and I scour the Black Friday ads and eat our second meal—McDonald's—Steve returns to my apartment, tells me about his holiday. His aunt had asked if he was dating me and he also said no, just friends. He told me she said it was for the best. She didn't think he should be seeing someone who gave away a baby. "Those girls are really messed up," she had said.

Bitch, I thought, *I gave you a candle.*

I wonder if you had your first solid food today. If someone who loves you made silly faces as she pushed a baby spoon loaded with mashed potatoes toward you while you opened your mouth like a baby bird, accepting. If you were here with me, I would've ripped a tiny piece of turkey off my bagel sandwich, blown on a French fry, let you lick it.

I've been thinking about humans and how we nourish each other. Sometimes in literal, obvious ways. But we also nourish each other in what Mary Gaitskill calls "some important, invisible way." I think about how my sister road tripped with some girls she barely knows for six hours to stay with me when she knew I needed it. I think about how mom sent us candy because she isn't here to feed us. I think about how we ate cheap bachelorette food because it was all I have to offer right now. We are feeding each other in the ways we know how. I think about how I'm not feeding you and wonder if I can still nourish you in some important, invisible way.

Christmas 2005

I've missed the Pacific Northwest: the drizzle, the evergreens that blur into one long green stripe in car windows on the freeway, even people saying "freeway." They call it "the interstate" back in Nebraska.

I just quit the Olive Garden. It was on prom night: teens with their boutonnieres and corsages, their six Dr. Pepper refills, their two-dollar tips. The hostess didn't cut me when she cut everyone else so I printed my checkout, handed it to my manager, and walked out. I will need to get another job as soon as I get back.

But for now, I'm home for Christmas. I just want to listen to mom's Evie cassette while wrapping presents with my sister, eat a shit ton of fudge, and see how big you've gotten. Last night, my dad took us all out to eat as a family. While he drove to the restaurant, he pointed at a house lit up in colored Christmas bulbs. "I see some lights!" he said, which was a game we played when I was younger. We used to count who could spot more. It felt all wrong now, him acting like I'm a little girl, but I played along to indulge him.

It seemed important to him to remember me as I was. I let him win, pretending I don't see the houses lit up on the hill.

Today we are driving to see you in Spokane. I am wearing those khakis that I met your parents in. Karen is driving since I left my car in Nebraska and flew here. Joel came along too, because what else is he gonna do? He's wearing his wrestling sweatshirt; I guess he's pretty decent at wrestling. He's not a small, skinny kid anymore. In the past four months he's turned seventeen, filled out, and even has some stubble on his face. He still has those ruddy cheeks and that dimple though, a reminder that he's still my brother, even if I'm an absentee sister again.

Once we make it to Spokane, to Greenacres to be exact—yet another charm that drew me to your parents—I marvel at how chubby you are how your body has stretched and filled out in this short time, before I've even been able to make a dent in my furniture debt. Your mother is very pregnant now, and she mixes formula with rice cereal, which I've never heard of. She lets me spoon it into your mouth. It drips on your bib because you hold my gaze from your high chair.

On the way back, we listen to Carrie Underwood's "Before He Cheats" on repeat at top volume. It is so dark here on I-90 in the middle of nowhere, before the mountains, after the city. Karen's tire blows and we all get out of her car to investigate, as if any of us are equipped to handle this. We can barely see our hands, let alone the tire or the lug nuts. I remember my dad taught me how to change a tire once, in case I ever found myself in this situation, but it is my second situation like this and both times I've needed help.

I walk along the freeway until I find a mile marker, then Karen calls the police from her cell phone. It takes a long time for a cruiser to arrive because we're nowhere near a town. The officer shows up grumbling. He points his flashlight at the tire and says to Joel, "Son, you should know how to do this" because Joel is a boy who looks like a man. Joel kneels and turns the socket wrench to loosen the lug nuts as the officer instructs him. The officer doesn't tell me or Karen we should know how to change a tire, but he does tell me I should be more prepared. I am shivering in my flip flops in the dark December air where the light from the stars is so dim I wonder if the stars are even there at all.

We make it back to the suburban houses strung up with Christmas lights.

Joel says, "Dad playing 'I see some lights' with you."

I groan and roll my eyes. "I know."

What I know about parents and children is that we stay parents and children, even after the children leave. We are locked in our roles. Even though I am an adult—I have birthed and given you away, I pay my own bills (but admittedly can't change a tire)—my father views me as his ten-year-old daughter still. And I give him that, pretending I still want to play the game I did when I was ten, knowing its importance to him, that I stay who he thinks I am.

It's a little like us, locked in roles we don't really inhabit.

I am your mother, although I'm not. When rice cereal dribbled off your perfect lip, I whisked it away with the tip of my thumb without even thinking.

About Your Biological Father

I would feel better writing this if I had more to tell you. If I had been in love with him or even knew him in a way no one else did. But I didn't. I didn't love him, didn't know him in any special way. I knew only the most basic things about him. I knew that he carried a gun, even to the pool. He didn't make me laugh or feel comfortable. I knew he wasn't very happy.

I knew that he had gone to college for a few semesters but came home when he injured his foot and couldn't play sports anymore. I don't even remember which sport. I know he spent his days smoking pot and playing video games in his parents' basement. His parents made wine in their garage and had a wine cellar he liked to show off.

I know he was in love with a girl named Megan who worked at Nordstrom. I know because we went there once and they argued near a register while I busied myself looking at merchandise, inconspicuously, I thought. I knew he was using me to make her jealous, but I didn't care because I didn't love him, didn't want him to love me, just wanted to feel desired for any reason.

He was stockier and tanner than I was. He had brown hair and space between each of his teeth. He had a tattoo on his arm, might have even been barbed wire. He drove a truck and had a criminal record. I wasn't sure what was on it, and I didn't want to know.

When I told him I was pregnant he said, "Is it mine?" even though he took my virginity and knew it. The adoption agency's lawyer threatened to tell his parents about you to persuade him to sign away his parental rights. That's the only thing he and I had in common: a fear of being disowned.

I don't even remember where I met him.

I wish I had more to tell you. I wish I could collect a bouquet of charming facts about your father and present them to you. But instead, this is the story. The hollow story. This is all I know of your father: he was nothing to me, and I was nothing to him.

He disowned you in a parking lot, signing his name where neon flags indicated on a document titled "IN THE MATTER OF THE ADOPTION OF INFANT DOE HMP (A Minor)." The document starts, "I realize that it is not in the best interest of the above named child to reside with me."

When my mother asked who the father was, I said, "A guy named Kyle." When she asked if I would marry him, I guffawed. Two hollow people cannot fill each other. We are not nesting dolls. We were still living inside our parents' hollows. I would push you into the world and at the same time fall from the nest that had cradled me. I would run away from the world I knew, the disappointment I had created. He would stay, without consequences or repercussions. In the world I knew, a guy like him carried a gun while a girl like me roamed around unarmed.

Pulp in My Hand

On the crest of a very tall cliff is a small house all my own. It is shaped like the crude box houses I drew once, when I was your age. Across from my cliff is another one with another house, another me. At the beginning of the dream her window is open and she waters what grows in her window box. Petunias. I never wanted petunias, but she isn't me, just another version who only lives when I sleep. I walk toward my window to get a better look at her, but I trip over a misplaced shoe. Even in dreams I am graceless. When I look up, her window is closed. I can't see her through the glass. It is milky—like a Midwest windshield in winter.

I know even without seeing her clearly: she is the me who kept you. I watch her figure move through the frosted window, from here to there, maybe fixing you a sandwich and washing the knife and then braiding your hair. I can't see you but I know you are in there. It tingles under my skin. Our proximity charges through me, turns my blood into an electric current. You are reading a book maybe, lying on your stomach, your ankles crossing and uncrossing.

I want to see the me who is your mother clearly. See what became of her. The peaks we live on are so close that I could touch her hand with mine if she reached through her window. I reach out mine, on my tip toes, stretch as far as I can. I grasp at what is there, snap a dangling flower from its stem. The pink petunia in my hand feels like skin. I would rap on the window if I could reach, beckon her to me. I want to see if her face is crossed with worry or if smile lines have crinkled her eyes instead.

And you. I want to see you, see if you turned out okay with me as your mother. I wonder if you've traded sparkles in for black yet. I want to know you, even if I am only guessing the person you are by what you wear.

But these cliffs create a deceiving proximity.

To see you would require me to pick my way down my cliff, then climb up yours. It would require a journey I haven't taken.

Instead, I stand here frozen by my window. With a cup of coffee in my hand, I watch your home on the other cliff. I watch the petunias reach toward the sun as the shadows move out and the dew glistens, then evaporates. I watch what grows around you without ever seeing you.

I watch until my coffee is cold. I look down into my other hand where I have squeezed the petunia so tightly it turned to pulp. Here, I should have a moment of epiphany. Here, I should realize your life and mine won't intersect. Here, I should realize what these cliffs represent. But still I am asleep. I drink my cold coffee down, quickly, to wake myself maybe. I stare again at the house where you live with the other me, the one who gardens and washes dishes immediately and knows what your hair feels like. The one who found a different way to live. I stare, wishing for something that isn't. That I never knew the life I didn't live, or that I knew it completely. That we lived on the same hill, in the same house.

Here, I wake up.

Grief is a mirror image of love, I read. We only call it grief after someone dies, but I'm stuck in between. Between the image and its reflection. Between grieving and loving a living girl I don't know at all. Mirrors create a deceiving proximity; I know this yet I keep thinking when I look into one I'll see you. When I look to see you as my reflection, there is only an opaque window.

II

Honeymoon

I got married on Sunday. I know people don't usually get married on Sundays, but the venue was half price. Steve and I wanted to leave most of my dad's money for this trip to Miami. I know people also don't usually get married so quickly, but no one seemed alarmed. Mom told Steve, "We're so glad someone wants to marry our Holly."

I could never afford this hotel except for my Sheraton employee discount. We didn't spring for a rental car, so we've just been hanging around the neighborhood.

I want to work out as a part of my married self. There's a gym here, but it costs extra. We tried running on the beach but we gave up after a couple minutes. I kept sinking into the sand and could never catch my breath.

Our first morning, we ate breakfast at the hotel restaurant. I got a lox bagel. It was expensive, even with the discount. So now we eat most every meal at Flanigan's Seafood Bar & Grill. It's only a couple blocks away, and they have TVs for him and seafood for me. They have this guy's bearded face on the sign and terrible green plastic cups and everything is fried, but we can afford it.

I wonder what it will be like to have money, to not always know the price of everything, to only work one job. Marriage, I've decided, is how I'll find out. Now, we are saving money on cocktails by drinking store-bought booze in our hotel room: whiskey (his) and Starbucks cream liqueur (hers). Married jokes.

Yesterday we went to the beach again. We walked into the ocean where the tide kept surging. After a minute, I returned to a chaise with a book. Steve stayed in the ocean. Then we went inside, back to bed, the one place we could agree on.

When I woke up, my skin was red. Burning. Burnt.

*

The night before the wedding, Mom ripped the seams out of the wedding dress I had bought online and resewed them to allow for my breasts. My sister bundled Calla lilies from Baker's Supermarket as my bouquet. I was thinking how if I had a girl—one I got to name, I mean—I'd name her Lily.

I took the shelves out of my apartment's refrigerator to fit my wedding cake (the bakery charges $110 to deliver it). On the morning of my wedding, I went to a budget salon without an appointment. I showed the hairdresser a picture of Avril Lavigne from her wedding last month: her soft waves. My hair didn't turn out like that, so I brushed it out. Steve drove to the venue while I balanced our cake on my lap, uncovered because that's the only way it fit in the fridge. "Don't wreck!" I said.

As I was getting ready—applying more eye shadow than usual for the occasion—I realized that although we had twenty bottles of $5 champagne, we forgot the orange juice. Karen sent her parents to buy me some at a gas station. I've never drank a mimosa so quickly and that is really saying something.

My sister played the keyboard as my dad walked me down the aisle. We stopped in front of the minister and dad gave me away as rehearsed. Then he turned to be seated, his part over. He stepped on the train of my dress by accident. To recover, he slapped his hand over his heart like a drunk pledging allegiance. "Oop!" he said.

Oop, I keep remembering.

*

I'm still in bed today. It's miserable here. I'm watching the news. Warren Jeffs was just captured. He's a polygamist. I don't know how he could handle sixty more women like me asking for aloe vera, pizza delivered to a hotel bed.

Last night Steve went outside to have a cigarette and met the Miami Dolphins' quarterback's brother. He relayed this to me, his voice rising when he got to the part that was supposed to thrill me. I scratched at my legs, willing my skin to flake off.

Today is the Dolphins' last preseason game, the reason we picked Miami for our first trip as man and wife. We bought T-shirts at Walmart to wear to the game. We both bought children's sizes. We took a cab to Sunlife Stadium in the middle of nowhere.

We got there too early, so we ate at Denny's where the cook wore a paper hat. I watched him slap burgers onto the grill, wondering where he got his arm tattoos. My skin is flaking off and everything burns. The aloe vera doesn't soothe at all, even when my husband rubs it on my back, my legs, my breasts.

14 Emerald Lane

I am packing up our things, putting books and knick-knacks into boxes to move back to Omaha. When I agreed to marry Steve, I insisted that we move. Moving is becoming my thing. I think of it as starting fresh, like that's real. There's starting over, but never fresh. We moved here to Illinois, where his father is stationed and could get him a job. I was hoping for Colorado.

When we moved here, we followed our MapQuest directions to the apartments next door. Steve parked the moving truck and I said, "These aren't so bad!" The apartments next door were new and trendy, with brick facades and even a pond in the middle of the complex with a fountain. In the leasing office, the woman looked at us with one eye squinted as if we didn't belong—wearing our sweat-soaked clothes that smelled of gas station beef jerky. "You're at the apartments next door," she said, pointing to where I am now, writing to you. There are no bricks, no pond or fountain. But my address is 14 Emerald Lane and it sounds quaint. My address is all I tell people about this place, except my sister.

Our apartment is right across the street from Longacre Park though, and every day I run or walk the trail. Sometimes I run before and after work at the call center. I dodge the geese around the water, the kids near the playground, the teenagers near the baseball field. I run every day to be alone and breathe. We eat healthy and I'm only 142 pounds now, which is a size six but almost a size four. Steve was running earlier this year too. He even agreed to run a marathon with his boss. But he never bought running shoes and was just running in these Puma street shoes until he tweaked his knee and bowed out. I remember thinking, he can marry the first woman he sleeps with but he can't commit to a pair of $60 running shoes?

I've been listening to Julie Roberts on repeat, this song that wails, "I'm already lonely / I might as well be lonely alone." I sing it aloud in the car if we're ever driving together, but he doesn't notice the message, only when I miss a note.

Steve spends Sundays at Hotshots where there is a blond bartender who wears a silver necklace that falls gracefully into her cleavage. I know this because I used to go with him and sip on beer and feign interest in the football games, but I only paid attention to the bartender. I shopped online for a necklace just like it but couldn't find the exact one. She wears a tight referee shirt, unzipped to where her bra clasps in the front.

Steve plays online poker at night when he thinks I'm asleep, and he has online conversations with this girl from his previous life. He told her he shouldn't have gotten married. I read that with tears stinging, not because he doesn't want to be married to me but because I don't know him at all. I don't tell him I read through his Facebook conversations.

Every day I run a little faster, a little farther.

I work at a call center where I was hired on permanently after they tried me out as a temp. I make $11.52 an hour. People call in and ask what their dental benefits are and I rattle off "100% preventive, 80% basic, and 50% major." Whenever they offer time and a half to process dental claims on Saturdays, I take it. Then Amanda and I sit in the training room together with the radio blasting. Once we called in and got our song played—Fergie's "Big Girls Don't Cry"— giddy with power when we heard our voices on the airwaves.

Steve works as an auditor for the government, and I save all my checks, living solely off of his. Together, we are proud of how good we are with money. Last month, when we had to buy a new car, Steve wrote a check for a used Hyundai Accent with only 28,000 miles. He signed his name with a flourish, clearly proud to be twenty-five and paying for a car outright.

After a year of marriage, I can report that it's not that exciting. It's paying bills, letting the dog out, obsessing about weight, getting drunk. We went to D.C. in February for Steve's job. I've never been to that Washington before, just had my place of origin confused with it. We had plans to see the Lincoln Memorial, the Pentagon, and the White House, but Steve drank a pint of rum without a mixer at his employer's party so I had to cover his mouth with my hand before he said anything stupid, drape his arm over my neck, and drag him to the elevator.

In our room at the Ritz Carlton, his head lolled from side to side against that heavy headboard. I tried to sleep, but I kept wondering if I should call an ambulance. Finally, I did sleep. When I woke, there was puke all over the carpet on his side of the bed so I just covered it with the white comforter and called the front desk and asked for housekeeping to be sent up. I forced Steve to the subway with me, to see the sights, but once we were underground he said, "I don't feel good. I can't do this." At the Dulles airport, he misplaced our boarding passes. We scoured the airport and almost missed our flight. That was the excitement.

Last winter, there was an ice storm. The rain drops froze before they could drip and soon the branches were collapsing from new weight. The branches fell onto power lines and phone lines and the call center shut down. Unlike a snowstorm, nothing was white, but everything was damaged.

14 Emerald Lane is a second story walk-up. These stairs I keep walking down to throw things into the dumpster are fresh cedar. They smell like new beginnings, as cliché as that sounds. Last week I opened the door to walk outside and the stairs were gone. There were a couple workers hammering nails into boards who said nothing, just rolled some temporary metal stairs over and I walked down them to my car and drove away.

We went to a Cardinals/Cubs game in the city with people from Steve's workplace. We got shitfaced, of course, because it was sponsored and because we were taking the metro home. We after-partied at Hotshots where I looked for the hot blonde with the necklace, but I guess it wasn't her shift. When Steve went to the bathroom, a man came up to me and said, "I've been watching you guys and I just want to know how a guy like him ended up with a girl like you." He said it like it was a question, but without the question mark.

"He makes me laugh," I said, but really, I was just thinking of that one time when he smelled Nick's hair and I laughed when I needed to so badly. I didn't tell the man that now I sing sad lyrics so my husband can hear them, hoping he will decipher them, cheat on me, and then we can call it quits.

While I was throwing things out today, I went through the closet in our second room (the room where Steve gambles and chats online, the room we agreed we needed for our separate space). I found my wedding dress in the closet and carried it to the dumpster: down the new cedar stairs, across the parking lot.

When Steve got home tonight, he dropped his keys on the counter, sighed, then ruffled Tucker #2's hair. "Was that your wedding dress I just saw in the dumpster?" he asked.

I lowered my book. "What else am I gonna do with it?" I said, a challenge.

"Yeah, I guess," he said. Then he closed his eyes.

I picked my book back up, turned back to my page thinking, *god damn right*.

What I Kept

My grandpa died when you were nearly two. I was in town for Karen's wedding, so I made a trip to see you. My mom rode with me and Steve, the six-hour drive from my parents' home to yours. I had invited Mom in a fit of compassion. She was repeating stories of her father's final days on a loop. I scribbled poems about my grandpa into a notebook.

He was the least religious person I knew and the most compassionate. I took my husband to meet him once, before Grandpa's health got really bad, and he said to Steve, "I like your beard" and that was when I realized I liked his beard too.

When we got to your house, you and Ethan were playing on the floor. I read you stories; you sat on my lap. It felt natural, the way your heavy head dropped against my chest. When your mother gave me your photo album, you pointed to the picture of you and me and said, "Mommy." I didn't correct you.

My own mother talked to your parents, repeating the stories about her father until she tired of it. Then she talked about me, about how it was when I was pregnant, as if she knew anything about how it was for me. She had lived in the same house, but in a different camp. Her commentary was about me but did not include me in the conversation.

That night, I cried in your parents' basement, in that yellow guest room where a quilt your mother had made was draped over the bed. Steve hugged me, rubbed my back, whispered that he knew that wasn't how it was. I was constantly struggling between believing what people said and standing up for myself. I was easily deceived. Having renounced my religion that I had always thought was truth, I couldn't decide anymore what actually was.

Eventually, Grandpa's eight kids sorted through his belongings, divided them up, sold off what was left over. They sold the house and just like that, it was no longer my grandpa's. I cried when my mom sent me the MLS link. I've never returned to those twenty acres where I would roam each Thanksgiving. I liked to explore the creek, ride his four-wheeler through the field, hide out in the musty barn. I felt at home there: in a place that wasn't my home but had been my mother's once.

Back when I was pregnant with you, my world tipped on its axis. I worried about falling off, about being thrown out of favor forever. My grandpa sent me a note on purple stationery that must've been my grandma's once:

Hi Holly—

Your mother told us at Friday's dinner the news that you are expecting in August. I want to assure you that

> *the family will welcome you regardless of your condition. You are still my "favorite" grandchild regardless. Your decisions on your future are going to get harder but that is expected.*
> *Love, Grandpa*

I keep it tucked in a box of memories of you, alongside your birth certificate, the hospital bracelet I wore, every memento I never expected.

Active Mothering

So I'm a mother now. To someone else, I mean. A little boy, Brandon Jude. Although he is beautiful and sometimes sweet, I gotta tell you, being a mother is neither fun nor games. It's something closer to torture. And I just left the hospital today.

When I was a kid, I remember my mom and her church friends talking about the outfit they'd wear home from the hospital: a white pants suit—size two—and big gold earrings or something equally ridiculous. Personally, I'm wearing these hideous green sweatpants with slippers. My experience was not glamorous, not in the least.

To get discharged from the hospital, we had to go ask a nurse in the hall. When the nurse finally arrived to discharge us, she talked to me about taking care of myself, about the baby blues. She looked at my puffy eyes pointedly.

I cried on the way home and then I cried when I pulled Brandon's infant seat out and saw his tiny head slumped forward since we didn't install that stupid car seat properly.

It was past feeding time so I hurried Brandon up to his nursery and gave it a go on my sore, cracked nipple. He didn't like how hard he had to work to get anything out of my nipples that are too flat. My body is failing me now, it's not made for mothering.

Over the past two days, I decided I couldn't breastfeed and today I told Steve we would have to use formula. I told him this while big tears dropped onto my breasts and snot poured from my nose. Steve made Brandon a bottle and I fed it to him, envying the perfect nipple that bottle was blessed with.

I laid down to nap, but my crying deterred me. I brought a trash can to the side of the bed for my snot-filled tissues. I cried because of how hard this all is, and it's only day three.

Day four: total systems meltdown.

I barely slept last night because Brandon thinks night is day and day is night. At 9AM, I fed him out of my breast (I am trying again using a nipple shield the hospital gave me), and when he unlatched I saw two blood vessels pulled halfway through the hole in the plastic shield. He is literally sucking my blood.

At four this afternoon, while Steve was out buying groceries, I resolved I would make this breastfeeding thing work. I googled correct latches and tried to get him to open his little mouth fully around my areola rather than just gnawing at my nipple. It didn't work. At the seven o'clock feeding I found blood in the nipple shield again and I changed my mind about making this breastfeeding thing work. Every time I try, I am biting on this stress ball I used to keep on my desk at work. It looks like a globe, and it's now covered in teeth marks, even has some entire continents missing from full bites I took in the heat of pain.

I sent Steve to Walmart to buy a cheap manual breast pump. While he was gone, Brandon pooped and kept screaming because after I changed his diaper I didn't dress him quickly enough. Instead of dressing him, I wrapped him in a blanket and fed him a bottle.

When Steve returned with the pump, we tried to pump my engorged breast. But the pump shocked the hell out of me, my nipple. It sounded and felt exactly like a staple gun.

I cried hysterically. I felt like a bad mom for giving up on breastfeeding only four days into it, because everyone says breastfeeding is best for your baby and now I'm some sort of degenerate, giving my baby formula which is not best. But honestly, I'm also a little relieved at the possibility of never having another baby's mouth on my nipple again. We fed Brandon formula the rest of the night as my nipples leaked and leaked and leaked and leaked through bras and shirts and sheets and even the mattress pad.

Maybe it's the lack of sleep, maybe it's my broken nipples, maybe it's the baby blues. But I don't know that I'm cut out for this. Mothering, I mean. Maybe it has never been in me.

But on Another Note

It's not all terrible: mothering. Some of it is positively charming. Like when my son wraps his tiny little fingers around mine or when he rests his head on my breast. When his eyes flutter closed at the end of the day while I'm rocking him to sleep. The little smiles he makes, toothless. The way his eyes twinkle, the way his hair smells, the way he tries to hold his head up and see the world.

I like those parts of this relationship that otherwise sucks me dry.

In fact, those parts might even make up for the parts that suck me dry.

I feel, when I look into his eyes, that he loves me unconditionally and that is something I've never felt. I've never been loved 360 degrees. It feels like even when I fail him, which I have (ahem, breastfeeding), and I will, my son will love me regardless. He needs me now, so his love does have a condition I guess, but one day, when he's your age, for example, I think he will love me all the way: for who I am, not for what I do. I wonder if you would too, had I kept you, raised you, rocked you to sleep, watched your eyes flutter closed at the end of each day.

I can't help but wonder: if I can do this for him, could I have done it for you? Did I deny you what I didn't believe I had when all along it was inside me, dormant? These what-ifs could drive me crazy if they let them. Instead, I'll try my damnedest to clear my head. Jewel is singing lullabies, and this room is dark, and this rocking chair is calming, and it feels like my eyes could flutter close if I let them. If I let them.

About Chains

There is something I don't know about mothers and daughters—something I don't understand.

I am twelve. I'm on a swing, clutching the chains with each fist and I am pumping my feet out-in-out-in, higher, higher, higher. My mother warns me about a kid who swung so high he flipped himself over the bar, knocked his teeth out when he hit the ground. This story is supposed to scare me into safety, but becomes aspiration: to be a kid who swung so high she passed over. At least the kid without the teeth has a story to tell. Not like me, this homeschooled kid in suburbia.

My mother had her two front teeth knocked out by monkey bars when she was ten. The fake ones she wears have turned black at the edges where they meet her gums. She has the scars on her knees, and I look at them in admiration, imagine them back when they were wounds still, when she was a child I think I would've liked to know.

I have no idea of what she was like at ten, but I've seen a picture of her at sixteen when she was the beauty queen in her little town. She rode in the parade atop the rear of a convertible, waving delicately, chastely, in a tight short dress. I love this picture of her when she was someone else: someone before Avon Christmas sweatshirts, before she was someone who only asked for spatulas for Christmas.

She used to sew and bake pies for the fair. She won blue ribbons in 4-H for the incredible wife she would inevitably become. They were bred for breeding, those farmers' daughters, the ones who knew that mouths needed feeding, bodies needed clothing; the girls who milked cows and hoed strawberry rows but knew little of crafting careers and following desires.

Back then, she was a model. She told me how she would have to line up against a wall and flatten her body completely. That's what models looked like: straight lines. She was "swaybacked," meaning she had an ass before asses were popular. She asked her father for a butt reduction, but he said one day you'll be glad for it, people will want a curve like yours. Her body was an upside-down question mark, not like the others: exclamation points minus the excitement.

What I know of my mom now that she is a wife and a mother is this: she sits in this large green checkered chair, a brown stripe on the back from hair products, and she scratches her head and reads the newspaper. She doesn't scratch at an itch, she scrapes her scalp with her fingernails, drawing up white residue she later picks out of her nail beds with a straight pin. It drives me crazy, her scratching, even the way she reads the newspaper. She reads the sports page—although she has no interest in sports—the business section, all of the boring stuff.

We don't tell dad that while he is at work educating kids, she sleeps until nine, and we're not allowed to wake her before then. When she is awake, if it's sunny, she lies on her Minnie Mouse beach towel, lathered in baby oil, from eleven to two, when the sun is best. She is so tan we don't look related. She barely eats, which worries me. Occasionally I see her eating a rice cake and I want to add a slice of cheese to it.

She was born into this life, but she doesn't belong here. She belongs on the back of a convertible, waving from a distance at people who admire her without knowing her. That's the girl I want to know, the one I don't know at all but feel I could understand, the girl who was blunt enough to ask her father for a butt reduction, a courage I could never muster, an honesty I was chasing. No matter how hard I try, I cannot flip my swing over the bar. My teeth stay intact. I can't find my story.

I am my mother's daughter and what I don't understand about mothers and daughters is how we are separate bodies but somehow, turn out so much the same, despite our best efforts. Our mothers' lives are self-fulfilling prophecies of our own future selves or they aren't, but the similarities are startling: how we laugh loudly, how our eyes crinkle, how we chase what we wanted or we resign ourselves to what we didn't.

I am thirty-four now. Here is something new I know about my mother: before I was born, she left my father. She moved back to her parents' home, with my older brother, age two. While I grew inside of her, she worked in her uncle's convenience store, eking out a life that was meager, but her own. I picture her stocking cookies on a shelf, the sandwich cookies she called "beach cookies' because her mother always bought them on the way to the beach. I picture her, thinking of the beach, the place she loves more than anywhere else.

Maybe it's the cool ocean air, the way it smells, how it hangs low and sure, clinging to her skin, becoming her. Maybe it's the sand between her toes, the gritty earth. Maybe it's just the thought of being with her family when she was young, before she married my dad and moved to a place that wasn't home. (Gracie, you must see our similarities, me and her). Probably that is it: the her-ness she had once, on the beach, before she became a wife and then a mother, fulfilling needs beside her own.

But you know how this goes.

I grew and she swelled and one day in March she felt labor pains and called my dad because she had to. I was half his. What kind of person wouldn't tell her husband that his daughter is being born? My dad showed up at the hospital. I have a picture of Mom holding me, my dad leaning over the hospital bed at an awkward angle, expendable. But he wasn't inessential, as the picture suggests. Over the past few months my mom realized she couldn't do it: raise two small children on a convenience store salary. She returned to my father's home, my brother in tow, me wrapped in a pink receiving blanket. She cemented her life with him and never tried to leave again. I am the daughter who forced her back to him, away from herself and her beach cookies, away from her family—and into his where she never felt at home.

What I know now is that I am not the black sheep of the family because of you. I got pregnant and brought shame on my Christian family, sure. How could anyone look at me the same way, knowing I'm an animal with sexual desires, one who doesn't even think to use protection? What a whore, what a slut, what a godless creature I am. But much before you, Grace, I was different from my siblings. I was the one who trapped my mother. I am not the black sheep as much as I am cement shoes. I always felt the weight of myself. I knew I was the slump in my mother's shoulders by how she talked about me, exasperated.

I've asked my mother about her own mother and she didn't say much, just said that she was really good at doing things with the girls in the 4-H club. Then she was quiet, and I remembered Mom saying she won 4-H ribbons for her sewing and cooking. I thought about my church ribbons and cringed. The two of us, confusing accolades for affection. Thinking we can earn love, that it's like gaining respect. We are perpetuating love in the way we learned it.

I never wanted a daughter. I know that sounds harsh, and I cringe to write this to you. I'm having a physical reaction to these words. I'm squinting, so I don't have to see them fully. But I couldn't shoulder reading in my daughter's diary one day, "I HATE MOM!" in all caps, the words my mom read in mine. I didn't want to live with the bad blood a mother and a daughter share. I didn't think that I was strong enough for it. I could not bear what I can't understand about mothers and daughters, how we resent each other for being alike.

When I was a kid, I knew if I had children, I would only want boys. My sister and I would giggle into the nights, writing each other's futures (a yellow house with a gingerbread trim, a chocolate lab). She learned to write me with two boys, because if she didn't I would ball up the paper she wrote it on and insist she write me a new one.

When I was pregnant with you, an obstetrician asked if I wanted to find out your gender. I was pretty close to sure I would place you for adoption, but I hadn't yet committed. I wanted to find out that you were a girl first. I thought it would make it easier to give you away. I laid there on that crinkly examination room paper, clear jelly smeared over my large belly while a woman pressed a wand over it, searching for a picture of you on the screen. You came into view: grainy, black and white. A lump grew in my throat the size of your fist when I saw you. No matter what gender, you were mine, and there you were, a giant head and a small body, the way I had been once when my mom stocked shelves.

"Are you ready?" the ultrasound technician said, and I nodded because I couldn't form a word, but the nod was a lie. I wasn't ready, I wouldn't ever be. I would never be ready for a baby, probably, but certainly not then. I was not prepared to be a mother to you or to anyone. I was still figuring out how to detach from my own mother, how to live on my own like an adult without blacking out or getting knocked up.

"It's a girl!" she said.

Relief did not wash over me. Instead, a tear dropped from my eye onto that paper, quietly but discernibly. I hoped the technician didn't notice.

I nodded again, wordless.

Then, as you know, many years later I had two boys, like my sister had predicted with coercion. But I wasn't fulfilled like I thought I'd be.

Last week, I was with my friend who has two ten-year-old daughters. "I want a daughter so badly," I said. It's a thought I have held for so many years but have never said aloud. The same thought I was having when that tear dropped onto the paper on the table when I was twenty weeks pregnant with you. Even if she writes that she hates me in her journal and we fight over everything, I want her, I thought. I want to watch her giggle with her friends before school. I want to pull her hair up in braids, tie them in ribbon. I want to listen to her tell me about the boys and girls she likes or just watch her eat her peas in silence while I imagine what she doesn't tell me. I want to sit side-by-side in spa chairs and get pedicures while we flip through magazines stained with nail polish. I want to buy her first bra. I want to cry uncontrollably at her wedding. I want to tell her all that women can accomplish and watch her prove to me there's even more I forgot to mention. I want her, I want her, I want her. I want the daughter I wasn't.

My mother has a beach house now. She shares it with her siblings: they measure out the weekends on a calendar, dole out days. On her weekends, she packs up her car and drives straight to the beach after work, without my dad. She meets her sister and they paint the walls or pick out knick-knacks for the rooms, trying to make it into somewhere they can feel themselves again. Although I have never been there, I can imagine it: the sheets smell of laundry detergent and they are overly thematic: the stripes in the pattern matching the paint on the wall, in the same color scheme of the tiles on the floor, pulling in the shade of the lamp. Mom must have it matching, the way our home was decorated in the nineties, the way she puts together packages she sends me, thorough, full of subtleties she hopes someone interprets. This beach house is a place she shares with her first family, the one who made her, not the one she made.

That one day as a kid on the swing set, the chains of the swing leave an imprint in my hands, not just dents, but also a smell, a smell I struggle to describe because it smells like a tinge, a cast, a stain. It smells metallic, the way blood tastes. The metal links felt so strong in my hands then, at twelve, too strong to break, so instead I tried like hell to flip over the bar, pass to another place, another story, one I didn't know, one I wasn't destined for.

There is so much I don't know about mothers and daughters. I don't know why we shy away from loving each other fiercely, why we keep each other at an arm's length. I don't know why we flail against becoming them. I don't understand the unsaid competition, the ways we try to show each other up as if one must be better, that we can't both be enough. I don't know why we aren't honest with our mothers, why we equate their approval with respect. Respect is earned in honesty, even if that honesty is raw and hiccup-filled and dropped as a disappointing bombshell. I don't understand it, certainly can't explain it, but I can smell it on my hands.

Ten

It's been six years since I've last seen you. And still, I wasn't ready. I wasn't prepared to see a tall blond girl who is nearing adolescence.

Today was the first time I thought of you not as a kid, but rather as a future adult. You are turning ten next week. While you played with Brandon and Holden, your mom and I talked about remembering ten. I remember visiting my dad's fifth grade class: I wore a hand-me-down Mickey Mouse shirt with matching turquoise jean shorts which I thought was a cool outfit before school and then afterward wanted to burn. I remember it was around ten that I began writing.

Even though the sun was still rising, it was so hot. We were all sticky with sweat. You aren't accustomed to Nebraska, neither am I, even after all this time. It's never become home, never felt right. Even still, you didn't complain. You paid attention to Brandon as he talked to you about animals and a show about animals, *Wild Kratts*. There was a moment when you and Brandon grabbed hands, when you helped him down the stairs that I thought my heart would explode out of my chest.

It was seeing you here, in a moment of my life, an ordinary morning like any other that made it all seem possible, the life I didn't choose. I thought about the room in my house we don't use, the big one over the garage, and thought how you could have it, paint it, draw skulls all over it for all I care, just be in my life and my sons' lives and let us have you in the ordinary moments, let us be in your presence for more than this one morning. But I could think that because it is only now, finally, ten years later, that I can give you what I never could before: a home, my time, my attention. Plans for our future.

It wouldn't have worked, this alternate life, because time didn't match up. I was too young, too unprepared, too distressed. I wasn't who you needed. You were who I needed but I couldn't commit to you. Somehow, within a year, I committed to a man, told him the rest of my life was his, but I didn't do that for you, my own flesh and blood, the baby who grew inside of me for nine months. I can't say why I did it, except maybe the hole in me after I gave you away left me so desperate to fill myself back up with something, someone.

After an hour, when the sun was higher, it was hotter, we were sweatier, and we got into our cars. You into a minivan with your family, me into my SUV with mine. We drove away, down the same road. When we veered off in different directions, I began to cry.

Ten

I had lost you all over again, and I felt your absence so deeply after being filled up. And then, from the backseat, Brandon said, "I miss Gracie," as if reading my mind.

"I do too," I told him, so sad I couldn't put words to it, still can't.

But there was something else there, too, beyond the sadness: this one morning, this one hour, I had been full.

Now I know it is possible.

Now That I'm Being Honest

I wore a long black sweater to Christmas dinner, 2004, to cover you up. You weren't visible yet. Maybe I had just the tiniest roll over my pants that I could attribute to college weight, but to me, my belly was already huge, stretched to accommodate my giant secret.

We sat around the table, spooning mashed potatoes and green beans onto our plates. Mom gossiped the way moms do about kids we used to know, ones who didn't turn out as their parents had planned. She clucked her tongue about a girl from church who was pregnant out of wedlock. I looked at my roommate across the table, the only one who knew my secret.

That Christmas, the long sweater was my shield. You may have learned already, as a daughter, the ways we protect ourselves from our parents' anger and protect our parents from disappointment. We learn to lie: to tell only parts of the story or to make up different stories altogether. Or sometimes we sit silently at the dinner table, chewing green beans.

I was raised to be quiet. "Children don't speak unless spoken to." I was educated at a kitchen table, from thirty-page workbooks with Christian comics as page headers. Learning a specific kind of morality was paramount to my upbringing. I was sheltered from the beliefs that weren't ours, from the people who weren't like us, from the television that blared sin in different shapes, from radio stations that played songs about sex. I spent my youth oscillating between my home and my church as if they were the only places on earth.

So many times I wished I was born into a subservient body. How much easier life would have been if I could just follow. But I was not born to obey.

"One need not write in order to have a voice," I heard once. But it was only in private writing that I felt allowed to speak as a child. I asked for journals with locks and wrote down my resistant opinions, my unspoken outrages, my dreams of turning into someone else. I carried my secrets on lined pages, stuffed them behind my shoes in the closet.

While I sat at that table, my parents didn't know about the nights I'd blacked out from too much alcohol. They certainly didn't know that I had lost my virginity that summer, after taking a shot every time Kyle blew something up in *Grand Theft Auto*. He and I ended up in his bed where I knew he was leading me, softening me with booze, blurring my boundaries. I winced once when he entered me. I watched the ceiling. The next time I saw him, he said his mom gave him hell for the blood on the sheets. *Imagine the hell I'd get*, I thought. My parents thought I was their virginal twenty-one-year-old daughter who worked two jobs to pay her own bills and aced her classes. There, at the table, I decided I would schedule an abortion.

In a way, I wanted to preserve what they thought of me. Abortion could save me from shame. Shame and a life I didn't get to choose. One in four women have abortions but I don't know the statistics on how many women talk about it. One in a hundred? A thousand? That option was my only hope that Christmas. It gave me a plan, a place to look besides down. That choice was my way of staying alive, of making it from one breath to the next.

*

Because you were born, people often assume I am not pro-choice. They think what I wanted most was to save your life. But there is more than one life to consider. Calling Planned Parenthood that winter was my realization I had agency. You see, before that, I kept confusing choices for mistakes. I hadn't been raised to think for myself. So when I was faced with a decision, I thought there must be an order I didn't know to follow.

But in our story, after I scheduled an abortion, a girl from my college googled my father and told my secret for me. In our story, I returned to my parents' home, to obeying them once I couldn't escape shame after all. I decided to have you, but I didn't keep you, although my mother tried to convince me it was the right choice. I had learned what decisions were mine alone to make. I found you a family better than me.

Desperation dwells where there seem to be no choices, I know now. I know that after marrying the wrong person, after taking so many years to leave. I know that because I've felt backed into a corner so many times, felt over and over that I had to turn out like the woman I was raised to become. I used to think I was ashamed of who I'd turned out to be. Only now I realize that the shame was from staying quiet when I should have been honest, outspoken, outraged.

*

It's May 2019, and Alabama has outlawed abortions. Women are coming forward and giving voice to secrets they've kept for so long. They are sharing their abortion stories, telling the truth so women will continue to have choices.

So now it's my turn. I didn't abort you, true. But after I gave you away, I aborted the atonement baby my body made in the lonely ache you left. I had a secret abortion, right after visiting you on your first Christmas. I borrowed money from my then-almost-husband to terminate what I couldn't bear to tell him we had made. It was January in Nebraska, or maybe February. It was cold, and the woman who sheltered me from the protestors with signs saying "Abortion is Murder" outside of Planned Parenthood wore a parka. I don't know what else to say about it, except that I never told anyone for a decade.

I have regretted a lot of choices in my life but this was never one of them. I was too fragile to handle another child in my womb, with you so fresh out of it. I couldn't house a child who wasn't you. I couldn't play mother then. I was too broken, too spilled open, too empty.

"I'll be honest" is a phrase we say these days, as if the truth is unusual. And I know it to be, since I remember it being locked away, out of sight.

But times have changed and I have a voice now.

Here are our origin stories: I was born into a life filled with expectations rather than options. You were born as one of those choices I didn't make. Your loving family is the choice I did make. That choice was the best I could give you. The abortion I had after you was the best I could give myself. It was how I could stave off devastation, how I could make it from one breath to the next. I am writing to you now, when I have finally learned to be honest. And I want to tell you our origin stories don't define us. Our child selves and adult selves are not tiles from the Memory game that have to match.

The last time I saw you was summer 2015. It was a few weeks before your tenth birthday. I gave you a journal without a lock. For you to fill with your stories, with your becoming, with the choices you're allowed to make.

Leaving

I am lying here in the bed my husband and I have shared for so many years, and tonight he was kind to me and loving, and before he fell asleep he rested his hand on the small of my back and a tear dropped from my eye onto our gray sheets and I thought: This is all I have ever wanted, for someone to hold me.

I once kissed a man who cradled my face in his hands. I think of it often, how he lifted me up to him, pulled me in, let me rest my head. When he traced lines up my legs with his fingers, my body convulsed in delight, from being wanted and from also being cared for like that. I hope I feel that again one day.

Love is a word that I've never known how to describe so I hesitate to use it. But I think it means to care for someone the way they are but also for who they will become. Flaws, mistakes, strange phases included. We failed at that, Steve and I—at loving the alterations and transformations: the updated versions. We couldn't adapt. We could love each other as those young kids we had been but not as the adults we had become.

Steve and I are letting each other find our best selves now, alone, because we can't do it together. There is love in that, I think, a different sort: folding the hand, loving someone's absence when you can't be present.

*

Today, we went furniture shopping for my new apartment. Before, we ate breakfast at Village Inn. Brandon brought a Rubik's cube. Holden ate a spoonful of butter, mistaking it for whipped cream. I looked at them, these obnoxious, sweet, feisty, beautiful sons of mine, and I loved them so fiercely, right there in their presence.

What I didn't know before writing you these letters is that we can also love someone in their absence. The way I've loved you. Removed, but still a part of you, as mothers and daughters inevitably end up.

I distanced myself from you too quickly on that first day of your life. A lactation consultant came into the hospital room and said we should try you on my breast. "No," I said, "I am her birth mother, this is her mother," and I motioned to your mother who was there. Your mother who has been there every single day, caring for you, loving you in your presence.

*

There is no other word for loving from a distance, removed. It is also called loving.

*

That is why I cried tonight, when my nearly ex-husband rested his hand on my back. Because he and I are choosing to do the same as I did with you. We are choosing to let go of what we couldn't manage. Give up, some might say. But we are allowing each other a better life than we could offer one another. We are loving with a void, from a void.

*

I held you on my chest the day you were born. I held you like you were my own baby, and in that moment, you were. You wrapped your tiny fingers around one of mine and I cuddled you so close to me that I worried I would suffocate you. I rocked you while I wondered if I could do any of this: raise you or give you away. Then your mother walked in and looked at me, at you, at us, and backed away so slowly, muttering, "I'm sorry."

I held you out to her and she smiled, then took you into her arms, wrapped a blanket tight around you. We fell asleep in that hospital room: your mother on the bench seat beneath the window, me hooked up to wires and tubes, and you in the bassinet between us.

Two days later, you were no longer legally my daughter. The day my milk came in. The day I stuffed my bra with cabbage leaves.

I want you to know how I have loved you all this time:
With a void.
From a void.
Love in absence, not absent love.

Bilocation

You're old enough now to be one of them. Sometimes I look out at the room of students and imagine you there, sitting among them, chatting aimlessly or cracking jokes or listening intently. I know you're not there but, even still, sometimes I land my eyes on the quiet blonde at the back of the room, and without my glasses on, she could be you.

I've been coaching these students to write and perform poems for three years. I was offered the job the same day I received the keys to my own apartment after the divorce. I am better at this job than I expected I'd be. I am twice my students' age, but we get each other in some way. They trust me because I am not their mothers and I listen to their outrage. I feel like I belong here, not as one of them, but as someone who has found where she is useful.

Here's the best advice I've given to my students: write as if to one specific person. Don't worry about a broad audience. I tell them that I wouldn't say the same things to them that I would say to my mother. We show different sides of ourselves to different people, I say.

This is how I've learned to write in writing to you.

My students have been my conduit to communicating with you. I was so nervous to talk to you before I met them. They have taught me how to talk to teenagers, which is to say *like adults*, without diminishing their experiences, without talking down to them. I've learned that the best way to talk to any person is with care and attention and honesty.

While they write, so do I. I write to you, this person I don't know outside of her Instagram squares yet who I want to be my most honest self for. Telling you who I've been instead of your mother is the only way I know how to forgive myself.

Today, I asked my students to join me in writing their most honest selves. I know that's a lot to ask of a teenager. I know they are living as personas. These students attend a Catholic school. Most of them don't identify as good Catholics. They are hiding parts of themselves from school staff or from their parents until they graduate or longer.

I know too what it's like to live as a persona. First as a pious person, then as a sinner, then as a wife. Now sometimes as a mother or as a writer. None of these fully describe me, but I've let the small truth of them define me as if whole. It's a protection, a hiding.

By and large, my students write on the same topics week after week. Same sex attraction and depression and external pressure come up again and again. They share these aspects of themselves for the group without sharing the parts they're not ready to talk about.

When I wrote today's lesson plan, I was thinking about how we construct personas around the parts of us we aren't afraid of and then we harbor those tender unspokens. I was wondering what would happen if we fed those parts of us that starve. Maybe the power of truth-telling is unlearning shame and learning to fill that space instead with pride.

Today I asked them to share something vulnerable and new.

I went first. This afternoon, I told them about you. I told them that after being home schooled, I started attending a private K-12 with a strict dress code in tenth grade. I was called a lesbian by a football player, and I never told a soul because I believed it was something to be ashamed of. It was the first time I remember harboring a secret self.

I told my students I went on to a religious college and both lost my virginity and became pregnant my senior year. One of my classmates tried to have the university kick me out, saying I was setting a bad example. But I had a Creative Writing professor who stood up for me. She asked me to become her TA so it would be possible for me to graduate while I grew you inside my body. I told my students that ten days after you were born, I moved here to Nebraska. I have never returned home. I told them I found a new home.

After I shared that, we sat at desks and, while a playlist cycled, we fed our tender unspokens. The girl in class who previously told us she wrote a poem she will never share ended up sharing that secret poem. Later, I received an email from another student thanking me for my authenticity. We were all so honest with each other. In that room we were nourished. And you, Grace. Although you are at home in Washington, you were also in that room. Your name and all the compassion it means.

For fifteen years now you've been with your mother, and also here with me.

I Keep Meaning to Write
About the Day You Were Born

A birth mother doesn't say she *gave up* her child for adoption. We say we *placed* our children up, careful with our diction because giving up means something different, something we are trying each day to avoid.

When people ask why I did it, I feel like it's a trick question with no right answer. Despite my fierce urge not to explain, I sputter and say I wasn't the best person to raise you. That is the truest sentence I know and also the hardest to say. I am not the most capable mother to parent the child I made.

This was difficult to admit then, thirteen years ago. It still is now. I am not the best woman to raise you into someone who will be better than I am. I don't know what I mean by better. I think I mean *more forgiving*.

I am not good at forgiving. I am good at resentment and remorse. *Forgiveness*. I know the definition of the word but can't remember a time I've practiced it.

*

I have boys I kept, and I wonder if that is the universe's compromise with me: how I can be a mother without forgetting the girl I didn't keep. There were six Mother's Days between your birth and Brandon's: 2006, 2007, 2008, 2009, 2010, 2011. Nearly seven years I lived in the body of a mother with listless arms. I'm not saying in those years I tried to forget you, but I tried to stop remembering you. I could not forget you anymore than I could forgive myself for trying to.

I think forgetting and forgiveness are tied to each other, at least I hear people say, "Forgive and forget." I used to have an impeccable memory. I recited 132 Bible verses in four days once and because of it won a Huffy bike. Now I misplace my glasses, my keys, my phone each day. Sometimes my fingers shake, and I think it is the absence of you twitching through me. My body remembering that it held you once, cradled you in my womb, then my arms.

I remembered that on those six Mother's Days: how warm your little body was the day you were born.

*

The Catholics believe in penance for your sins, which I never understood completely. I am not Catholic, but *Sacred* was the first language I knew. Penance, I think, must be actions toward forgiveness.

Sometimes I wonder if all these trips to the zoo and the children's museum and putt-putt golf are my own actions toward forgiveness. Like I'm trying to prove that I can be a mother now that I wedged space between me and you. Like those six Mother's Days were me incubating, becoming for my boys what I couldn't be for you.

When I looked up *penance*, I read about self-flagellation. That's when a person punishes herself by whipping her own back. It is a voluntary punishment to atone for some wrongdoing. I wonder if writing to you—this unmanageable task of putting words to sorrow—is my self-flagellation.

I think what I'm saying is that I keep hoping you will forgive me.

When I first sat down to write to you, it was to exorcise this grief from my body, to pull it through my throat in long ropy blood vessels. I pulled and pulled until they pooled on the floor in giant piles: wet and heaving red cords I had never seen in the light. When I stepped back from them, aghast at all that had lived spooled inside me, it felt like I would never swallow again.

I've felt like that before, when your second half-brother was born. When the anesthesia wore off, I came to and wondered where I was. When I heard the cry of a baby, I winced, knowing a nurse would bring the baby to me and knowing I would hold the baby close to my breast—our skin steaming where we touched—and knowing it was temporary.

You see, I thought he was you.

*

I keep meaning to write about the day you were born. It's been a task on my office whiteboard for months. But when I think of how it felt to hold you and know I had forty-eight hours to change my mind, to keep you, it still feels like I'll black out.

I remember how small your fingernails were. How your mouth yawned open when you woke, how you rooted toward my nipple. When the nurses and the lactation consultant advised me how to feed you, I kept explaining that I am not your mother, just your birth mother. While they refilled my ice chips and shuffled around on the polished floor with squeaky shoes, I lay there holding you, as if the slow speed of you opening your fingers would be how time worked for us.

For those deciding hours, that's how time moved. Only the hours I slept were quiet. All the other ones, my mind turned over keeping you—over and over, over. Not one of the scenarios I constructed were feasible. Feasible maybe, but nowhere near ideal. For either of us, I mean. The feasible ones had us in my parents' basement—my family babysitting you while I worked a shitty job or two trying to get ahead. The feasible ones had me gasping for air outside of that house, just like I had been doing while you grew inside me. The feasible ones had you passed around from person to person who wasn't your mother. I wondered if you would wait for me to get home and coo at long last in my arms or if you would believe someone who held you more than I did was your mother. If it would be like that, I'd rather find for you the mother I couldn't be.

Which I had. She was next door, waiting out forty-eight hours, hoping to God I wouldn't change my mind.

*

I don't think I'm going to write that essay about the day you were born after all. I just wrote what I could. There are parts I can't tell you because they can't be pulled from my body. They have melted into my throat, retreated into the lining of my womb, settled into the bones of my feet.

I can tell you that I had to get out of that hospital as quickly as possible. I had to wait out the rest of those hours away from you. Karen picked me up from the hospital and we went to a movie. *Must Love Dogs*. It was brainless and stupid, and I kept looking down at my hospital band, wishing I had cut it off.

It said *mother* on it.

*

Sometimes I see snippets of your dad's sermons on social media and think about how weird it must be to believe in god. I mean, I did too once, I remember. I fell asleep to Jack

Hyles' sermons on cassette when I was your age, went to a Regular Baptist Church.

Fundamental means forming a necessary base or core of central importance.

My mother told me to apologize to our church for making you and I said, "Don't you mean ask God for forgiveness?"

That wasn't what she meant.

When I moved away from home, ten days after your birth, I left everything I knew behind. Including my religion. I wouldn't say I lost it as much as I abandoned it. What I believe in now is friends who let me cry into cocktails while I give voice to all this I never said before. Now I believe in the pursuit of forgiveness. In the endless grasping to be good enough, to be loved, to be understood, to feel okay.

*

It's hard to get all this in when someone asks, *why'd you do it?* It's difficult to articulate to anyone who can't imagine giving her child away that I also couldn't imagine giving my child away. Sometimes people like me end up in circumstances we never thought we would. I gave you away and I haven't given up.

I initially ended that last sentence with *yet* but I deleted it.

I deleted it because I know I won't give up now. I didn't know that at first. I didn't even know it a decade later. But in writing these letters to you, I'm coming to some conclusions. For example, that I am forgivable. I am making a church of healing people, building a sanctuary with words. I am doing this without forgetting you.

I am remembering you more than I ever allowed myself before. I see the shape of your newborn fingernails in the silt on my keyboard while I type. I remember your young, earnest voice that time you called me on the phone. I can still hear it all these years later. I remember the space between your voice and mine.

I remember that I had both nothing and so much to say.

There Was Joy, Too

Maybe it's strange to start here, but when I began to chronicle my joy, I first thought of a day with my now-ex-husband, after many years had worn on, when I got stoned with him in our backyard while our kids slept upstairs and his laugh was so contagious and his smile so authentic that I thought my own mouth would split like a halved orange from smiling too hard.

There were days when I drove through rural Nebraska towns and watched the birds overhead flying in Vs or settling onto electrical wires and I named the clouds.

There was the day I got a good deal on a new bike, when the employee named the price for my smile when I rode it.

There were days I understood the value of my joy.

There were days I realized the value of myself, without having to be told.

There were days I reminded myself that I have something to give and I am giving it.

There were days I didn't try to find my identity in someone else.

There were days I didn't wear a persona as if it was my own skin.

There were days with my MFA friends when we stayed up until two a.m. talking about books and religion and erections and we laughed so hard, scribbling in our notebooks words we would never decipher.

There were days I jammed about writing with my students and they shared the most heart-wrenching, beautifully put-together sentences. My skin prickled and my eyes filled as I walked out of school with my headphones on, filled again with good.

There were days when I took selfies because I liked the way my eyes twinkled in the sunlight and I posted them to my gallery as another image I could smile about later.

There were days my sons played charades with me and Holden gave away the answer when we couldn't guess, saying, "It's black and white and lives in China and is a bear."

There were dances in the kitchen while sausage sizzled.

There was coloring for the quiet of it.

There were reunions between me and Brandon when he said, "I want a hug" and threw his body against mine in collision and didn't let go of my neck until I pried his sticky fingers from my skin.

There was the day I made a YouTube playlist with my girlfriend called "LOL" so when our sadness returned—which it would—we would have somewhere to look for joy again.

There were moments at the art museum standing in front of paintings or marveling over the grain of the wood floor.

There were days when I noticed how my skin felt, wallowed in my taste buds, swallowed wonder again and again.

There were days that I didn't think my writing was terrible and I wrote and wrote and wrote. When the sky darkened, I boiled water in a kettle and made myself an apple cider, then settled back into the navy of my desk chair, enveloped in words.

There were days I wasn't so self-assured but I submitted poems to literary journals anyway.

There were days I wrote letters to my friends in colorful ink, thankful for companionship, for secrets spoken—hushed, urgent—in libraries.

There were days I listened to the same song on repeat through my headphones, fifty times, and never grew weary.

There were days I was kissed, pressed against my car, when I felt wanted.

There were days I prepared three meals for my boys, when I felt needed.

There were days when I wasn't kissed and got takeout instead of making food, and as I walked up the stairs to my apartment door, I inhaled deep breaths of the corridor air, enamored with the smell of achieved independence.

There was Tampa and L.A. and New York and Brownville and Chadron and Laramie: travels with my best friend where we drank too much and gossiped and read stories and drank some more.

There were kind text messages I read again and again.

There were days I walked around shopping centers, buying assorted trinkets and clothes and candles in colors and textures and scents that spread my lips giddy.

There were Thanksgivings and Christmases in Puyallup when my brothers and I played Mario Kart on the N64 for hours, growling when our kids wanted to take our controllers.

There were dinners alone with glasses of wine and deep bowls of Beef Bolognese where I found meaning in the flame of the centerpiece, the gait of the server, the hunch of the woman in the corner booth.

There were flowers I bought for myself, stalks standing tall in a vase.

There were flowers my sons picked for me which floated, stemless, in the water of a mason jar.

There were days I didn't have to get fucked up to remember how good things can be.

There were movie theaters with buckets of popcorn and Brandon's explosive laugh that sounds like a cartoon character I want to watch on a loop.

There was mud squeezing between my toes, snaking up my feet.

There were runs through pine trees when I stared at the brown needles beneath my feet and thought about home, what it is. I wondered if it could be there in my pounding chest, if it could be the wind in my lungs, if home could be the constant running toward a better someone.

There were shed skins: better versions of me that came after worse ones.

There were tears of nostalgia rather than sadness.

There were used bookstores that smelled of already read pages where I spent all the cash I had, down to the nickel, balanced paper bags threatening to bulge out of my arms on the walk to the car.

There was a Murakami novel devoured in my reading chair while the boys giggled laps through the sprinkler.

There was a long wait at a trendy restaurant when I read a short story aloud, in love with words and that person who looked at me like nothing else existed, not even the wall behind us.

There were days I stared at the ceiling and didn't want to move, not because I was depressed but because I was content.

There were days I stayed after the restaurant closed and had drinks with my managers, gossiping about our co-workers, paying no attention to tomorrow.

There were laughs at the coffee shop with my co-workers that spread so wide I couldn't calm myself enough to take an order through the intercom.

There were days I didn't think of the empty I cradled.

There were days I didn't try to fill a void with booze or

compulsions but instead turned on a CD and practiced yoga and later underlined my favorite sentences while I read.

There were days when booze or compulsions felt like joy instead of a temporary filling.

There were days I didn't think I should lose weight or didn't tell myself I'm a bad mom, days when I didn't agonize over what people might think.

There was the day Dan and I almost broke up, both of us nursing our separate pains, but we talked about our dreams instead and discovered them the same.

There was so much tenderness. Gracie. I'm telling you, there were people who were gentle with me. I melted into the sweet of their words, the warm of their arms, the beat of their own joy. I let them hold me on days I couldn't prop my own self up.

There was joy, so much of it.

I remember now.

There was joy, and it was full and robust.

It bloomed as full in me as my emptiness sprawled vacant.

I had forgotten to give it voice.

But in this writing to you, my howl became a song.

I Want You to Always Know What It Feels
Like to Be Held in Someone's Arms

I don't care to list the ways my mother has hurt me.

I have no intention of making a list.

This past weekend, I took my boyfriend Dan back 1,700 miles and fifteen years to Puyallup, where I was raised, where I grew you while I harbored every resentment against my mother.

There, the room went cold and hard when my mother and I shared it.

After the family dispersed and my boys were asleep, I cried into Dan's chest—sobbed, really.

All I said between hiccups was "she was supposed to be the person to teach me love."

I didn't know if I was mourning my mother's failure or my own to you.

*

I recently fell in love with this man so kind and good.

Grace, I didn't know I deserved him.

I quit drinking shortly after I met him.

I didn't want to feed the sad animal of me.

Already it was fat and growing.

But there is something tender about loving someone new, and I think it might be the chance to tell my story to someone who wants to hear it.

I saw my mother twice this year.

Once last weekend and once in June.

In June, she told me she's proud of me for my sobriety.

I don't know if that's the first time she's told me that, but it felt like it.

I said I wouldn't make a list, but she called me selfish for giving you away.

She thought the only reason I would do that was because I wanted to be free.

She had no idea how alone I was during your growing, after my giving you away, in the empty of my first apartment, in the first year of marriage and then all the subsequent ones.

Maybe I don't understand what freedom really means, but I didn't think that had been it.

Was this selfishness? I wondered. Giving you what you needed and hating myself?

*

If I were to make a list of everything I wish for, a daughter would be at the top of it.

I mean you of course.

But knowing that is not an option, I've started daydreaming a baby falling asleep in Dan's arms.

We gave her a name last summer in Minneapolis, even though we know it won't happen, but I have to have this hope because it's hard to swallow what I won't have.

I credit you for my ability to dream.

You made space where there wasn't before—I mean this literally yes: you expanded my belly and made room for new life, but I also mean you grew my capacity to love.

*

I have found myself so curious of my own mother.

I try to find ways she and I are alike, but more exciting discoveries are ways we differ.

If I had kept you, would I have resented you the way she resents me, or would you have resented me the way I resent her, or both, or none of the above?

Today your dad posted a family picture on Instagram and my god, Grace, you look so grown up.

You look like me but also different.

I wonder if you too are curious about your mother.

I think I'm writing this book in the hopes that you are.

I've always struggled with feeling good enough.

I read Kelly Corrigan's book where her father tells her, despite her screw ups, she is good enough, and it seemed like the most radical thought.

I think growing up in a religion where there was good and there was evil meant I didn't consider all the middle parts, and of course the middle parts are where I live.

I always believed I had to forgive or be forgiven.

I know now that isn't it at all.

Being loved this year, so tenderly, so completely, despite all my screw ups has reinforced this idea that I am worthy of good things.

I know this writer who is also sober, and when I couldn't keep my mind and body straight, I reached out to tell her about my self-loathing. I couldn't keep it to myself anymore. She said not to talk about myself that way; if I wouldn't allow my friends to talk about themselves that way, I wasn't allowed to talk like that either.

*

I keep finding women who resemble mother figures.

I had a visitor at my graduate reading, Tonie, who drove from Chicago to Omaha and sat in the front row.

This past year, Tonie died.

Before that, she and I made her daughter a website, which she wanted to finish before she passed, though she wouldn't have said *passed*; she would have said something like *croaked*.

She showed me a mother's love could mean spending your final days making sure your daughter is set up for all the success you could possibly give her.

When the pandemic hit, Margret taught me to knit.

She gave me metal needles that I didn't know how to hold, and she stood behind me, curling her body over my body, her hands, knobby from age and knitting, poised over mine.

She doesn't have a daughter.

When we went to the library book sale, she told the librarian she wished I was hers.

*

When I was pregnant with you, Grace, I wanted most to be mothered.

I've kept wanting to be mothered all these years since.

I wasn't mothered immediately; I haven't had that in the conventional way, but I've made do.

There are people who love me in ways that are similar.

People have been taking care of me.

These past few years I have been perfectly cradled.

I know you don't remember when I held you.

That was a lifetime ago, before your memories started.

I want you to always know what it feels like to be held in someone's arms.

It's hard to say it doesn't have to be from me, but I've learned it doesn't.

What matters is that you are held.

I know you are now.

And later, if ever you feel you're not worthy of it, let me put it here in writing for you to read as many times as you need until you don't only remember it and repeat it, but you believe it.

You, baby, are worthy of every good thing.

Acknowledgements

I am so grateful to the following publications who first gave home to my words before they became this book: The Rappahannock Review ("The Pet We Never Shared"); The Nasiona ("About Chains"); Jellyfish Review ("Now That I'm Being Honest"); Pussy Magic ("I Keep Meaning to Write About the Day You Were Born"); Moonchild Magazine ("Pulp in My Hand"); Porcupine Literary ("Bilocation"); and Autofocus ("Honeymoon" and "Say You're Pregnant").

Thank you first to Grace's parents who gave my daughter everything I couldn't. Thank you for loving her into this beautiful ferocity she continues to become.

Thank you to Michael Wheaton for seeing this book for what it could become and ushering it all the way there. And to Amy Wheaton for your gorgeous art to finish it.

Thank you to Jen Ippensen and Mike Keller-Wilson. "Friend" isn't a word expansive enough to include all you have been to me. There are so many writers who read my early drafts and gently nudge me toward better ones. Jen and Mike of course and also: Barry Glynn, Jim Kourlas, Jessica

Anne, Tyler Michael Jacobs, Travis Cravey, and Ashy Blacksheep. Thank you a thousand times over.

There have been many people who have offered me selfless kindnesses when I needed them most. They include: Lenae Nofziger, Karen Weingartner, Joel Pelesky, Julie Curtiss, Rolly Dietel, Amber Johnson, Reed Halvorson, Tonie Harrington, Margret Kingrey, Gina Tranisi, Jenn Pohlman, Roger Slatten, Rebecca Rotert, Tammy Brown, Kristen Deane, and Rachel Brodsky. You might not have known your kindness was the exact thing I needed, but I did.

There are also a handful of people who are no longer in my life in the same way they were, but were a big part of me and the making of this book. Mentioning them by name wouldn't feel right anymore but that doesn't make me any less grateful for their part in my becoming.

There are so many writers whose work I have admired. They have influenced my own craft, broadly or very specifically. Thank you for not only creating art but perpetuating it.

Brandon and Holden, thank you for recognizing me as your mother and an artist and for cheerleading me to be both, often at the expense of your own attention.

And to Dan, who loves me not despite of all I am but because of it. Thank you feels too small a sentiment.

About the Author

Holly Pelesky writes essays, fiction, and poetry. She was once a homeschooled kid living in the suburbs of Seattle but has spent her adulthood in the Midwest, outgrowing her Fundamental upbringing. She received her MFA from the University of Nebraska. She works in a library, coaches slam poetry, and raises four boys with her partner in Omaha. Placing her daughter up for adoption will forever be the hardest thing she's done.

also from Autofocus Books

Duplex — Mike Nagel

XO — Sara Rauch

Until It Feels Right — Emily Costa

Nextdoor in Colonialtown — Ryan Rivas

Too Much Tongue — Adrienne Marie Barrios & Leigh Chadwick

Picture Window — Danny Caine

the nature machine! — Tyler Gillespie

A Kind of In-Between — Aaron Burch

How to Write a Novel: An Anthology of 20 Craft Essays About Writing, None of Which Ever Mention Writing — ed. Aaron Burch

Hiraeth — Mistie Watkins

That Spell — Tate N. Oquendo

My Modest Blindness — Russell Brakefield

A Calendar Is A Snakeskin — Kristine Langley Mahler

Culdesac — Mike Nagel

Razed by TV Sets — Jason McCall

In the Away Time — Kristen E. Nelson

The Body Is A Temporary Gathering Place — Andrew Bertaina

Daughterhood — Emily Adrian

Leave: A Postpartum Account — Shayne Terry

Yes I Am Human I Know You Were Wondering — Erin Dorney

A Healthy Interest in the Lives of Others — Teresa Carmody

Out There in the Dark — Katharine Coldiron

Organic Matter — E.N. Couturier

If I Can Be Honest: Selected Prose from the Four Years of Autofocus Lit (2020-2024) — ed. Michael Wheaton

Marginalia — Naomi Washer

A Revisionist History of Loving Men — Lena Ziegler

The Dead Dad Diaries — Erin Slaughter

The Third Beat — Lauren Lavín

Tacoma — Aaron Burch

Teen Queen Training — Kristine Langley Mahler

www.ingramcontent.com/pod-product-compliance
Lightning Source LLC
LaVergne TN
LVHW040105080526
838202LV00045B/3784